Guardians

THE HALI'A ALOHA SERIES

Guardians

CATHERINE BACHY

LEGACY ISLE
PUBLISHING

THE HALI‘A ALOHA SERIES
Darien Hsu Gee, Series Editor

Hali‘a Aloha ("cherished memories") by Legacy Isle Publishing is a guided memoir program developed in collaboration with series editor Darien Hsu Gee. The series celebrates moments big and small, harnessing the power of short forms to preserve the lived experiences of the storytellers. To become a Hali‘a Aloha author, please visit www.legacyislepublishing.net.

Legacy Isle Publishing is an imprint of Watermark Publishing, based in Honolulu, Hawai‘i, and dedicated to "Telling Hawai‘i's Stories" through memoirs, corporate biographies, family histories and other books.

Grateful acknowledgement to Coleman Barks, translator of the quote from Rumi in the epigraph. Rumi, "Every Tree," in *The Glance: Songs of Soul-Meeting*. Translated by Coleman Barks. New York: Viking/Arkana, 1999.

All photos courtesy of the author.

ISBN 978-1-948011-85-3 (print)
ISBN 978-1-948011-86-0 (ebook)

Legacy Isle Publishing
1000 Bishop St., Ste. 806
Honolulu, HI 96813
Telephone 1-808-587-7766
Toll-free 1-866-900-BOOK
www.legacyislepublishing.net

Printed in the United States

Pour Philippe et Mireille,
mes parents

With life as short as a half-taken breath,
don't plant anything but love.

Rumi

CONTENTS

IV.

I.

FIRST LIGHT

I come from a tribe of women who are early risers.

My paternal grandmother, Georgette, would grind coffee before going to bed at night. "It's for the early morning," she'd say. "I grind it now so I don't wake you up. I will make myself my cup of coffee and sit here by the window and watch the lights of the fishing boats."

She liked to wake up in pre-dawn hours and sit on a stool in the kitchen and look at the ocean. In their retirement, she and my grandfather lived in a post–World War II apartment building in the Basque town of Hendaye on the French side. It was tucked away on a bay formed by the Bidasoa River and the Atlantic Ocean.

"On clear nights, I can also see the lights of the fortress of Fuentarrabía." Her hand would wave in the direction of the medieval fortress in northern Spain, perched on a cliff overlooking the Atlantic.

"I like to be alone with my thoughts," Grand-mère would tell me serenely, her hand rubbing the crease lines on her forehead. Her gaze would land in peaceful reverie on the ocean. "It's three, maybe four, in the morning, and I watch until I see the first light on the horizon. Then I go back to bed and sleep a couple more hours."

The first waking hour of the day, roughly between five thirty and six thirty, is my favorite hour of the day. I ride the last wave of dream time, that space before busy brain and to-do lists take over. If I am lucky, a line from my first waking hours will make its way onto the writing page. The voice from the world of sleep is like a rare rabbit, easily startled away.

In the first light, from my window I see a corner of my city awaking. I see the quiet caterpillar of the light rail car, its red and white lights glowing as it arrives at the station on the aboveground rail. I see the cars of teachers inching, snail-like, along my street in search of parking. They are here early, before the high school across the street fills with students. Are these teachers also hanging onto the inspiration of their calling and their hearts' longing?

THIS MOMENT

*O*dette and Georgette, Lille, 1928, is written on the back of the photograph. I recognize my grandmother's handwriting. The small black-and-white photograph looks like a frame cut from a film strip. It's a sunny, cold day on the bustling street in Lille, a city in northern France. My grandmother, Georgette, and her sister, Odette, face the photographer and smile. Behind them, a row of pedestrians gains on them. For a flash the two young women look like they are leading the parade.

They are twenty-two and twenty-four. My grandmother was the youngest of her five siblings. They are wearing winter coats and fashionable cloche hats. My grandmother's coat is unbuttoned in front, revealing a satiny dress.

"Sometimes we skipped a meal to save money for a new dress," I remember Grand-mère saying, happily reminiscing about the first time she lived away from home.

Odette and Georgette are far from their ancestral village in southwest France, where they were born and grew up. They have passed their administrative exams and are qualified to work in the post office system. They are telephone operators, plugging lines into a vast panel, connecting people voice to voice, to family, to doctors, to places of business. They have side-stepped marriage for an opportunity to be on their own and make their own money.

Soon, they will meet their future husbands. Within a decade they will each have one child, but they do not know this now. The saber-rattling of war is distant and easily ignored. They have no inkling yet of the loss that awaits them.

DEER IN THE HEADLIGHTS

She remembers the hunger, how horrible it felt in the pit of her stomach to not have enough to eat. It's the only memory she spoke of from that time.

My grandmother stands out in the black-and-white photograph. *Georgette.* She is next to her uniformed husband among eight other uniformed men in the photo. She is wearing a fur coat, black and velvety, that matches the shine of her short, wavy hair. She looks glamorous against the brick government building in front of which the group is posing. The men wear crisp uniforms and boots. French military insignia adorn their sleeves and collars. They are lieutenants, medical officers, conscripted in service to the new Vichy government, now under Reich orders, since the German soldiers marched across the North of France in 1940.

They look as if they are in costume, ready to act in a play. These are not the costumes they usually wear.

It could have been worse, is written in the creases of their stunned eyes, the stiff lines around their tense smiles. Or possibly, *We are the lucky ones.*

In a few months, my grandmother will board a train heading south into unoccupied France with her five-year-old son, the boy who will one day grow into my father. She will find safety for him with her sister for a while. "It's just until things settle down," she will say to him.

She'll return without him, to be with her medical officer husband. They will count their ration tickets and hope to have enough for a chicken to put in their pot. At some point she will have a nervous breakdown. But we never spoke about that.

SUZANNE

At the corner of my paternal grandfather's vast physician's desk was a small, framed, sepia-toned photograph of a toddler. It looks out of place amongst the piles of medical journals, prescriptions, and scribbled notes. It is not immediately evident in the photograph that this child is a girl. She is not wearing a frilly dress, or a bonnet. She is at the shore, walking in a low outcropping of rocks. She is wearing a black swimming costume like the ones that people wore in the early 1900s: a black shirt with three-quarter-length sleeves and a pair of black shorts. Although tiny, she is steady on her feet. She holds one hand out as if to keep her balance. Strands of silky hair blow around the delicate features of her face. She is the only figure in the photograph. No one is holding her hand. She is gazing towards the photographer and also keeping an eye out in front of her. In the background, the slope of land leads to the shore of a body of water, the banks of a lake or of the sea in the North of France.

On the back of the photo are the words, *"Suzanne Bachy, 1915–1917,"* in my grandfather's handwriting.

She is his little sister. He would have been eleven years old when she died.

"Your grandfather loved the little Suzanne, *la petite Suzanne*," my grandmother whispers when we look at the photograph.

"He grieved her for a long time," she continues. "He always kept this photograph nearby. There was one in his study and one in his wallet. He never talked about her."

I remember another photograph. It's of my grandfather at ten or eleven. He is wearing knee-length knickers and socks. Suspenders stretch across a white short-sleeved shirt that is buttoned all the way to the top of his collar, at the base of his neck. A camera attached to a strap around his neck rests at his waist. He is holding it in a way that suggests that he knows how to use it. I wonder if it was my grandfather, young Jean, already bespectacled with round glasses, who took the picture of his little sister, that day at the shore. Is it his reassuring voice that she hears as she delicately steps around the rocks?

Dr. Jean Bachy was a serious man. Most of the time his reserve seemed impenetrable, like the metal boxes where he kept his sterilized instruments. The rare glimpse of his emotional life, his tenderness, was the picture of his sister, always nearby. He never talked about her. He did not share how she had died. At the time, it was not out of the ordinary for children to die of common illnesses. Was she his reminder of innocence? Was she the private angel he kept near as he traveled into the dark places?

FAMILY PORTRAIT (1942)

Antoinette is holding her Sunday hat against her leg in the photograph. She is twelve or thirteen, the only one of ten siblings who has a hat. Bernard, the only boy, is wearing his tie over his short-sleeved shirt. He's ten. This was a rare occasion. I pick out Mireille, my mother, who is maybe five, and squeezed on a seat next to her mother. The photo is part of a feature story in a regional French newspaper. I recognize my grandparents, Papé and Mamé, sitting on wooden chairs from the kitchen. They are surrounded by their children. The older ones stand behind them. The younger ones sit on laps and tuck under arms. The mother is resolute. "The family is complete," she is quoted in the article.

I wonder how long it took to get everyone dressed in their Sunday best to pose for the picture. How long did the photographer have to wait for noses to be wiped, tears to be dried, and smiles to be coaxed forward?

Even during World War II, a family with ten children was newsworthy. They were awarded the Silver Medal. They didn't set out to be a poster family for the Vichy Regime's nationalistic motto: *Work, Family, Fatherland.* The medal had been an honor. No prize money was included for an extra pair of shoes or a bar of chocolate, or for layettes for the two babies who would follow.

Years later, her husband has died and the children have all moved away, and the original framed photograph hangs on the wall in Mamé's sitting room. My cousins and I stare at it and point out our parents. We giggle. They are so tiny.

II.

I AM

From a young woman arriving
on a ship named *Le Liberté*
as she, Lady Liberty, rose up
on the horizon of a foreign world.

From a young man seeking opportunity
in an enchanted land.
Cigarettes burning in ashtrays,
trays of dishes delivered to the upper class.

From lullabies sung in French
Langue maternelle. Mother tongue.
From bewildered listening to the hard,
Anglo syllables learned at school.

From elbow grease and taking risks,
from worry about meeting payroll
during a snowstorm that
shutters business for a week.

From La Fontaine and Molière,
from Shakespeare and Thoreau.

Memorized poems and piles of homework
from working hard to get ahead.

From languorous, loud dinners for twenty
under the acacia tree on the terrace
where cicadas sing all summer long
on sunbaked Mediterranean days.

From three kisses alternating cheek to cheek;
visits to aunts and uncles and
cousins I only saw every few years.
From saying goodbye more than saying hello.

From misty eyes when I hear "La Marseillaise"
sung in the Olympics or for Bastille Day.
From a lump in my throat under "The Star-
    Spangled Banner"
and taking a knee for the dream of "justice for all."

From hiding and awkward sentences
to avoid revealing the gender of my lover.
From doors shut and conversations ended
when truth is revealed.

From sewing quilts to honor the dead
lost to a disease that dared not speak its name.
From Marches to forge a road of equality
and from Pride Parades to celebrate the living.

From staying up all night to care
for a dying father.

And not sleeping through the night
to rock my baby with lullabies sung in French.

I am daughter
I am granddaughter
I am niece
I am *cousine*
I am sister
I am wife
I am friend
I am mother.

CHANCE MEETINGS

How did my mother, Mireille, a nineteen-year-old non-English-speaking immigrant to the US, leave her first employers, French diplomats, and find another job at the British Embassy? Did she just walk up to the British Embassy and ask if they were hiring? Knowing what I know now of looking for work, I am awed by my mother's nerve and courage to leave the cocoon of her French-only nanny job and find another job at the British Embassy.

She worked in the kitchens there, helping the chef with the *mise en place*, cleaning and peeling vegetables, whisking sauces, stirring pots. Mireille had moved from the French diplomats' home and found her own studio apartment on the bus line to the British Embassy. On her days off she went to the lunch counter at Woolworth's on Dupont Circle and ordered a BLT, her favorite American food. The salty fat of the bacon and the juicy tomato slices tasted like freedom.

"I remember when the famous British Prime Minister came to stay at the British Embassy," my mother reminisces now. "You know, the one from the war. He met with Roosevelt and De Gaulle." She is searching her memory for the name, as she often does.

"Do you mean Churchill?" I offer, flipping through my memory's Rolodex of famous prime ministers.

"Yes, Churchill. He was a big man. He would sneak into the kitchen at night and help himself to leftovers in the walk-in fridge. One of the other girls saw him. She hid because she didn't want him to see her."

My jaw drops as I imagine my mother's co-worker hiding around the corner and watching Winston Churchill helping himself to a midnight snack. And then running to share this with the other girls in the morning.

"You met Churchill?" I ask in surprise. Why hasn't she shared this with me before?

"I didn't meet him really. He was just there. And, well, he loved to eat!"

Mireille met Philippe, my father, when they were off work with other young French restaurant workers.

"We met at Dupont Circle," my mother recalls.

Dupont Circle is an elegant traffic circle in Washington, DC, containing a neoclassical marble sculpted fountain. On a hot day, passersby can sit along its wide edge and enjoy the cool mist from the fountain. It's in the middle of what is known as Embassy Row, a street lined with embassies from all over the world. I have walked through Dupont Circle many times. It's been a popular gathering place for a hundred years. It's now a gentrified, upscale neighborhood and part of Gay DC.

I imagine my mother hanging out there with other "girls" from the British Embassy or from other restaurants and meeting young men who wandered over after they finished their restaurant shifts. They probably smoked cigarettes because that was fashionable then.

"We would just talk and share stories. We'd laugh. Sometimes we'd go out for a drink somewhere," my mother pauses and gazes into the landscape of her memories. "If we stayed too long and if there were too many of us, the police would come by and wave their baton and tell us to move along," she recalls.

Wow, I think. *A dozen or so young non-English-speaking adults hanging out enjoying the cool mist of the fountain on a hot evening, how threatening could that be? Did the police think they were communists, planning the next revolution?*

FIRST WORDS

Sounds reverberate in the womb, vibrations of fear or love. First words heard in the light of life: in cold or warmth. *Fais dodo*, lullabies to rock to sleep. *Fais dodo*. Home was one language, intimate cocoon, or isolation.

The two girls in the stairwell have red and mean faces. Their voices are loud. I am frozen in fear as they taunt and grab my tricycle. Maman is putting away groceries. She runs back down the stairs and scoops me up to safety.

It took a while to make friends. How did I decipher the sounds coming from their open mouths? I watch and listen.

"She is such a shy girl," teachers said. "She barely says anything."

It's not as if I was raised by wolves, like Mowgli. Still, the whirl of words is dizzying. At first, I invent words. Add an extra syllable or sound to a French word. Friendship and kindness don't require words: offer, gesture, parallel play.

Smile.

Connection.

Silence.

GEOGRAPHY LESSON

Catherine, age 8; photo by Helen's father

I am eight years old, and I live in Rockville, Maryland. We speak French in our house, so sometimes it seems like we really live in France. Helen is my best friend and next-door neighbor. Her parents are from Germany. Helen says that her father goes to work in Germany every day.

When I ask my mother about this, she says that Helen's father goes to Washington, DC, to work in a camera shop. She says Germany is too far to go to every day.

"You can't get there by bus," she says. "Just like your father," she explains, "he goes to Washington, DC, too and he works in a restaurant."

When I tell Helen this one day, that her father does not go to Germany to work but to Washington, DC, just like my father, she does not believe me.

"No," she says. "My father goes to Germany."

I decide not to argue with Helen.

AGE OF INNOCENCE

We wear matching jumpers in the picture. They were the ones we wore to the pool over our bathing suits. They are red, made from Basque fabric. The traditional white embroidered designs land around our waists on the jumper. They are sleeveless. A zipper runs up from knee height to the top of our breast bones. We lived in these jumpers in the summertime. Our mother had made them for us, back when she sewed our clothes. We had several matching sets of dresses or skirts, little suits. Sometimes they were different combinations, variations on a theme, and cut out of the same cloth.

I remember the day this photograph was taken. It was hot in Maryland, and we were going to spend it at the pool with Maman. On our way, Maman drove us to Sears. We went to the photo department in the back. A man in a blue polyester shirt with a name plate over his pocket greeted us. He arranged us behind a table that had a piece of beige carpet on it. My forearms felt scratchy leaning into that carpet. *Carpet on a table, that's weird*, I remember thinking.

We are sitting close together, your shoulder against my chest, my arm tucked around your back. I am eight or maybe just about to turn nine. You are three, almost four. Our hair is parted in neat, straight lines down the middle of our heads. Your brown hair is pulled back into two wavy pigtails on either side of your face. My curly hair is pulled back into a ponytail; fuzz escapes from the barrettes on the sides. My hand rests on yours lightly. Your smile looks frozen, just as it did when you were about to giggle uncontrollably. My teeth are barely visible under the slight part of my upturned lips. I am not quite sure if it's okay to smile. In my gaze, I detect a hint of skepticism. Was it the seriousness of the older sister beginning to show?

That was before I cringed in the mirror at my uncooperative hair. Before I covered my mouth with my hand to hide my two big front teeth. Before we were concerned about being cool or popular, or having perfect bodies.

LITTLE DOGS

Milou

"Milou" is a common name for dogs in France, made famous by the *Tintin et Milou* comic series. My Milou, my first love, was a wiry-haired terrier my parents' friends brought when we moved into a house. I was almost five, and apartment living was all I had known. Running through seemingly endless empty rooms with Milou chasing me was a freedom I had not experienced.

My mother was emphatic that dogs lived outside. "*Dehors,*" she told us. "*Un point c'est tout.*" "Period." I already knew the stories of Boby, the family dog when she was growing up with her ten sisters and one brother. Boby ate kitchen scraps if he was lucky, and he slept outside.

I let her half-scolding voice, directed at everybody and nobody in particular, drone on and slunk away to the backyard with Milou.

When I was nine years old, my parents announced that we were all moving back to France. "All" included our familiar things. I watched lamps, books, paintings, records, all our clothes, get packed into trunks for the trip across the Atlantic. But not Milou. He was not coming, and I was devastated.

"Why can't we take him?" I whimpered.

"Because it's too hard for him to travel to France," my mother said.

In the weeks before we left, I couldn't walk past Milou without curling up next to him on the floor and burying my face in his soft, curly fur and crying. I hoped that one of my parents would have a change of heart.

"Your grandparents can't have dogs," my mother offered as another explanation.

My parents, my four-year-old sister, and I were going to live with my grandparents in the city of Poitiers. I understood "can't have a dog," as "didn't want a dog."

My grandfather had recently had a heart attack. He was retiring early from the medical practice he ran out of the stately family home. My father, the only child, felt the vast distance of the ocean between himself and his parents. He decided that it was time to move back to France.

On the day before we left Rockville my father took Milou away before I was awake. I had said my final goodbyes the night before. I was resigned now.

"Papa took him to live with a nice old lady, who doesn't have children and is lonely. He'll keep her company and she'll take good care of him," my mother tried to reassure me.

I wasn't sure whether to believe her. It sounded like a fairy tale with a happy ending. I wonder if I'll ever really know what happened to Milou.

We settled into our new life in Poitiers. My grandfather's operating room, where he had recently performed outpatient eye surgeries, had been converted to my bedroom. The operating table had been replaced by a bed surrounded by bookshelves. The linoleum floor made a funny sound when I walked on it. It was a room trying hard to be cozy instead of sterile.

Within a week I took up my campaign for a dog. It was all that was missing, I explained, from our life in Rockville. There were lots of dogs in France. And there was lots of room in this big house. I would take care of the dog, walk it, and feed it. The adults did not budge.

As the hope of a new dog faded, I found religion. By religion I mean Mary, the Blessed Virgin Mary, the mother of Jesus. I attended an all-girls Catholic school where one nun taught all the subjects. The only time she seemed to enjoy teaching a room of thirty nine-year-old girls, was when she talked about Mary. I started going to church on Sundays, even when my parents weren't up for it. I walked to the cathedral in the center of Poitiers. I sat on the wooden pew and knelt on the well-worn kneeler, surrounded by the permanent smell of incense from hundreds of years of smudging. I talked to Mary. I shared my worries and disappointments. She was a very good listener. I always felt better afterwards and walked back home with a bounce in my step.

At home, my parents and grandparents were in a quiet tug of war. My father looked grey with exasperation as his parents second-guessed his every business instinct. Six months into the return to France experiment, my parents let me know that we were going back to the United States.

It was dinner time. We were sitting around the table after dessert.

"Yeah, I knew that," I told them in a quiet, even voice.

"How did you know?" my father asked.

I looked into his warm, brown eyes, "The Virgin Mary told me."

"The Virgin Mary?" he asked.

"Yes, I talk to her and she told me."

Nobody spoke for a moment. My parents gave me that "you never know about this one" look, both loving and dumbfounded.

My grandmother, the stubborn realist, guffawed, "Great, we'll have a plaque installed at the cathedral in Poitiers, in your honor," she said sarcastically. "The Virgin Mary appeared to Saint Catherine here."

I just looked back at her, certain in what I knew.

Amos

By late spring we were settled back in Maryland again, and my pursuit of dog ownership resumed. This time I scoured the classifieds in the Sunday paper for ads of puppies for sale. I made phone calls to inquire on various possibilities. Finally, I found a promising lead and my parents agreed to travel to Virginia, a bit of a drive away, to check out this dog. We were met with a litter of irresistible beagle puppies. I picked one out and we drove home with him in a shoe box in my lap. I remember how cute he was. I gently stroked his soft fur. He peed all over the box. I had a sense that I had my work cut out for me.

I named him Amos. It was a biblical name, it turns out. I didn't know this when I chose the name. I found out on a Sunday morning at church, when the priest introduced the first reading, "A reading from the prophet, Amos." My head snapped up and I glanced down the pew at my mother. Our eyes met and we burst into a fit of church giggles. Every time I thought I had my giggles under control, I would sneak a glance at my mother and notice her shoulders bouncing up and down, her chin tucked into her chest, her face red. That would set me off all over again. I'm sure we each peed our pants a little that morning.

I was right about Amos being a handful. He gathered up my sister's stuffed animals and buried them one by one in the backyard. I managed to train him to lift his paw and shake. We never got to the more practical, "come, sit, stay."

One evening after dinner my mother and I were doing dishes at the kitchen sink. She washed, I dried. My sister was watching a show on TV. We became aware of the sound of a baying dog, a howling we had not yet heard out of Amos. In the dim light of dusk, we realized that our dog was no longer in the backyard. We hurriedly dried our hands and went outside to search for him. We found a hole and a tunnel under the fence. Amos was on a joy romp through the neighborhood. We headed out, treats in hand, to retrieve him. When we eventually found him, I picked him up and carried him home. He was euphoric. That was pretty much how it went with Amos. He'd disappear and then we'd hear the distinctive beagle baying signaling his wild chase.

Amos lived through two more house moves. There was never a question of whether he would be included. Miraculously he lived to become a fat old beagle who could no longer go up and down stairs.

"After Christmas," my mother confided, when I was home after my first semester of university, "I'll take him to the vet and have him put down."

"*Pauvre bête*," she continued. "Poor animal, he is suffering. This is no life for a dog."

He was a good dog. We had a chance to say our goodbyes.

Fiona

More than a decade of big life events passed. I moved across the country with my life partner. My sister got married. My father died, leaving my mother, at age fifty-eight, to face an empty house and the overwhelming task of reimagining her life without him by her side. Then a new dog snuck onto the scene.

Fiona was a chihuahua puppy that my sister adopted. She was an infusion of cuteness and joy into the world of her two young daughters. They called her Fifi most of the time, but Fiona suited her too. As my sister's life got full to overflowing, and the girls spent more time at school, there was not much time for Fiona. The dog spent increasingly more time at home alone.

My mother got involved. For better or for worse, she "helped out" at my sister's house. The boundaries of "help" and "control" got blurry. Soon her attention was drawn to Fifi's well-being. She talked to her. She fed her treats. She complained to my sister that Fifi was lonely. (This is when I am glad I live three thousand miles away, outside of driving range.) After months of this kind of "help," one day Fifi went home with my mother.

"I was walking to my car, and I looked back and there was Fifi at the storm door window, watching me," my mother explains. "She was looking at me as if begging me to take her home. I went back to open the door and Fifi walked down the front stairs and headed straight for my car and hopped in."

That's my mother's version of the story. It's convincing, especially to her. I don't know my sister's version of the story. In any case, this was the beginning of a joint custody arrangement that seemed to work out for the dog and the people.

Fifi mostly lived at my mother's house, a twenty-minute drive away from my sister's house. When my mother was away, Fifi would go back to stay with my sister. Over the years, my mother's scolding, "*Non. Non. Non,*" persisted at the hint of a crouch on the carpet. She would pick Fifi up and put her on the newspaper she had laid out. In time, Fifi earned a spot on the couch for daytime and a little bed on the floor in my mother's bedroom after Fifi's advancing age and girth made it hard for her to jump up on the bed.

Fifi became a fat and cranky chihuahua. She growled at everybody except for the people she knew and trusted: my mother, sister, and nieces. When I visited from Seattle, I approached Fifi with caution. Her growl set clear boundaries. My mother fed her steamed broccoli and shared a bite of her morning toast with her.

My sister and I would catch each other's gaze and mouth to each other in English, "Who is this woman?" when we observed my mother's fawning over Fifi. What ever happened to the woman who insisted that dogs slept outside or at least in the basement? Even though this doting attention had us raise our eyebrows and smile, we preferred this version of our mother.

In February 2021, during the COVID pandemic, Fifi took her last breath.

"I knew something was wrong," my mother told us. "I checked her bed next to me and she wasn't there, so I got up. It was three or four in the morning. I went downstairs and found her laying on the kitchen floor. When she saw me, she got up and dragged herself to the little bed in the living room just around the corner. She was breathing with difficulty. She looked at me and I could tell she was trying to stay." My mother pauses. "But then she closed her eyes and she was gone."

Another long pause. I think that maybe my mother is crying, but I can't tell over the phone.

I imagine my mother as she tells me the story of holding vigil over Fifi in her last moments. She is only inches away from where she held vigil for her husband, my father, twenty-six years prior. She had a chance to say goodbye.

HER

I dreamt last night of pilgrim trails.
Walking
between small chapels in the back country,
secret pearls to the Black Madonna.
Walking
in the footsteps of the ancient ones,
in the footsteps of the plain folk
who revered signs of the Goddess,
long excommunicated from the canon,
not from their memory.
Walking
on hidden trails
devoted
to Her.

PORTKEY

In the United States, my family and I lived within an hour of Dulles Airport outside of Washington, DC. It was an unspoken criterion that each time we moved, we had to be able to get to Dulles Airport. My father would take us there on Sundays. We would go to the observation deck and watch the planes take off and land. He would lift me up on his knee and hold me there, standing on one leg, so I could see over the railing. He would watch the planes with the still attention of a heron. After a while I'd ask to come down so I could run around on the deck and make my way to each of the standing binoculars. They looked like large heads with two eyes and a round oval for a mouth, where a nickel would fit, buying a chance at being able to see into a plane's cockpit. It was loud on the observation deck. The planes preparing to take off revved their engines to high-pitched squeals. It was windy. Sunbeams, reflecting off metal wings, made me squint as I fixed my gaze on each plane. When we had taken in all that we could of the wind in our hair, and when our ears had had our fill of engines roaring, we'd go back inside and visit the snack bar. My father would buy us an ice cream or a Shirley Temple.

It was the same snack bar we would go to when we brought my grandparents back to the airport to see them off after a visit. We'd have a snack with them before saying goodbye. Then we'd walk with them all the way to the entrance of the shuttle they would board to take them to the airplane. We'd wave. I'd keep watch for them. I followed their movements into the shuttle. I'd follow them to their seats and kept them in my line of sight for as long as I could. The shuttle would slowly pull away and we'd make our way to the observation deck so we could follow them all the way to the airplane. My father would point out which plane it was, and we'd watch and wait. Watch and wait until the plane would pull away from the gate and lumber its way onto the tarmac and find its place in line for takeoff. It looked impossible, that this whale of a plane could lift off the ground and turn into a giant raptor. But it did each time. And then they were gone, back into the clouds. Soon they would cross over the Atlantic Ocean and in early morning hours they would land in Paris.

We would quietly walk away and make our way out of the airport to the parking lot to find the car. Each one of us, my sister, my mother, and my father, awash in our own world of emotion. I imagine that my mother felt some relief that the visit with her in-laws was over. My father may have felt some sadness to see his parents leave. He may also have experienced some ease from the watchful gaze of parents towards their only child. I felt sad and homesick. It was rare for my family to have family members visit us. My grandparents visited every few years. In between we would revert to our familiar French island of four inhabitants in a sea of Americans. My father would take us back to Dulles Airport on a Sunday afternoon so we could feel closer to the ones on the other side of the Atlantic, so we could remember that we could reach them. Like the magical places in Harry Potter's world that transport wizards across dimensions, Dulles Airport was our promise of reunion.

MULTICULTURAL NIGHT

Fifth grade, 1972. My parents accepted the invitation to make pastries for the Christmas multicultural night at my school. For weeks, my father planned what he would make. He settled on three items. *Tuiles* are individual rounded, buttery, caramel cookies that are made to look like the shingles on a roof. They take this shape after laying the warm malleable discs right out of the oven onto glass bottles laid on their sides. I was in charge of that molding process, my small, patient hands holding the warm, sticky dough in place. *Petits choux* are round puff pastries that fit in the palm of a hand. Each is filled with a custard—chocolate, coffee, or vanilla— and topped with a little puff pastry hat. I was not involved in these except to lick the empty bowls before washing them. Finally, the *piéce de résistance:* the *bûche de Noël,* or the Yule log.

The weekend before the celebration, my father commandeered our kitchen. With my mother, sous chef at his side, they turned out sheets of *génoise,* a fluffy light cake for the *bûche.* My father was not going to simply create a pastry that he would roll into a log.

He deemed that shortcut unworthy of his training in the Paris Hôtellerie Institute. Instead, he sculpted the log from precisely cut pieces of génoise and fastened them delicately together with a chocolate butter cream. During this process one batch of génoise was deemed useless and tossed onto the dining room table. My sister and I sampled it and found it quite to our liking. We ate it for breakfast, lunch, and dinner while our parents worked all day in the kitchen.

My father sent my mother out for butter several times. My sister and I had to go with her because my father could not keep an eye on us. He had to keep baking. I remember the bleary-eyed, sugar-induced fog while standing in front of the butter section in the supermarket. My mother examined each box carefully to double check the ingredients. At the supermarket in Maryland, it was hard to find the right kind of butter.

By Sunday night everything was covered in flour dust and crumbs. My sister and I had licked so many bowls of buttercream that the idea of butter now turned our stomachs. In the fridge was a magnificent bûche de Noël. My father had sculpted the bark of the log out of chocolate buttercream. There was a little mushroom made from a lightly toasted meringue. Gold leaf outlined a sprig of holly made of red and green buttercream. It was a feast for the eyes. We never did eat a slice.

The French table at the multicultural Christmas night in the school cafeteria was a folding table draped with one of my mother's tablecloths. She had decorated the table with two little French flags and sprigs of holly and greenery. The pastries were artfully arranged and dusted with a flourish of powdered sugar to give everything the gleam of freshly fallen snow. Set up on a platform, in the center of the table, was the masterpiece: the bûche de Noël. My father delicately cut the bûche and laid slices out on paper plates.

I wandered to other tables in the decorated school cafeteria. There were other cultures represented: German, Irish, Mexican, Italian. Many parents dressed in costumes representing the culture they were from. There were sombreros and lederhosen and women dressed in embroidered dresses and bonnets that made them look like life-size dolls. It had not occurred to my parents to wear cultural dress. They had not gotten that memo.

My father wore what he would wear to work at the restaurant: a dress shirt and tie, a pair of pressed slacks. He tucked the end of his tie in between the buttons on his chest to protect his tie from food splatters, his sleeves rolled up to his forearms. He wore a chef's white apron. My mother also had an apron over her dressy blouse and pleated skirt. She wore stockings and heels.

Looking back, I suppose my father could have worn a flashy chef's toque, or perhaps a beret and a blue-and-white-striped shirt, like a French sailor. He did not own any of these items nor would it have occurred to him to go out and find them. What costume could my mother have worn? A cancan dress from the Folies Bergères? A nineteenth-century bonnet? They came as themselves, not realizing they were being asked to be part of a multicultural show.

My parents looked stiff and uncomfortable behind the decorated folding table, where their exquisitely designed masterpieces lay. They held their mouths in frozen smiles, while visitors to their table loaded up their paper plates as if they were at an "all you can eat" buffet. I felt a mix of pride and protection. I was proud of my family and my parents and all we had created. We had done everything we were supposed to do for the multicultural celebration. Yet we arrived home quiet, tired, and feeling strangely out of place.

MOTHER TONGUE

"Hmf, deez peeshez are so hard. Not ripe." Maman has switched from French to English in the grocery store.

My sister and I steal cringy glances at each other. We are young teenagers, old enough to be mortified by our parents in public places. I move close to my mother in the produce section, so she can hear my loud whisper, "*Parles en français, Maman,*" I say, urging her to speak in French.

"Deez tomatoz are not ripe eeder." She gets in one more complaint before she switches back to French and gives me her squinted-eyes, stern look. "*C'est vrais les fruits ne sont pas mures.*" It's true, these fruits are not ripe.

It is an unspoken code. We speak French to each other unless there are English speakers around, then we speak English. The supermarket is tricky. We move our bubble of French through the aisles. Maman can complain all she wants; nobody understands her. But we are in English-speaking territory; the lines are blurred. Maman pulls rank and crosses that invisible boundary to share her displeasure with any English-hearing ears nearby.

At check-out, it's worse.

"Dees iz a long line. Iz taking soo long," she complains.

We are trapped. We can't move out of the line and lose our place. I remind her again in a pleading whisper, "*Parles français!*"

"I weel speek how I want," she snaps loud enough for the other people in line to hear.

Oh God. I wilt in embarrassment and become very interested in the magazines in the racks near the checker.

Maman rarely misses an opportunity to air her opinions. To this day, when we are in public, she breaks away from our French bubble and switches to English. I still flinch and look around to see if there are any judging glares turned our way.

III.

THAT GIRL

Is that a boy or a girl?
Cropped curly hair,
the athlete's sculpted back,
arms and thighs of lean muscle.
"Young man?" she hears the question from behind.
"Young man?" now louder, more emphatic.
Wait. Are they talking to me?
That girl turns around. Confusion spins in her eyes.
Brow furrowed on her smooth, twelve-year-old face.
"Me?" she asks in a soft, polite voice, pointing to
     her chest.
"What are you?" asks the lady in line behind her.

TURMOIL

That morning, I stumbled off the bus and into my twelfth-grade English teacher's classroom. Mrs. M. was the teacher I could talk to about feeling stuck between two worlds. She could hear my internal conflict even though I did not yet have the language to express all of what was churning inside. I had had an anxious night. I hadn't been able to sleep. I poured myself a brandy from the liquor cabinet. I thought a nightcap would help my chronic insomnia. Instead, it made me ill and starved me further of sleep. Mrs. M. put her arm around my shoulders and guided me to the nurse's office. I lay down on the bed, staring at the ceiling and softly crying. The nurse called my mother.

When my mother arrived, I sat up on the bed. She looked perplexed by my current state. This was unusual for me. I was a "good daughter," I never got into trouble. We didn't speak as I gathered my books and lunch. We were silent on the drive home. I felt nauseous and out of my body as we retraced the journey I had only recently made by bus.

At home I went to my room. I closed the door. I wanted to disappear. I did not want to be alive. I was scared.

My father came home early from the restaurant. I could hear their low voices in the kitchen where I imagine they were discussing the situation.

Nobody was yelling. That was a sign of serious concern.

By evening I didn't come to dinner. The last thing I wanted to do was to sit in the same room with anybody, let alone my family.

"Not hungry," I said, when my mother came into my room and perched on the edge of the bed.

"Is there something you need to tell me?" she asked in her worried voice. It was the first time she had spoken to me since she came to pick me up from school.

"Are you pregnant?" she asked finally.

"Nooooo," I groaned, turning my head to face the wall.

I had no words to talk about the deep truth of my attraction towards women. It was 1980. I didn't know any gay people. I went through the high school rituals of having a boyfriend, going to the prom. References to homosexuality or gay people were biting and cruel. How could I even begin to talk about the chasm between my growing awareness and the pressure to act in betrayal to the deep truth of my being?

My mother was quiet for a while and turned to leave my bedroom. Maybe she was strangely, though not completely, relieved. She could rule out one reason that might explain my current state. But the mystery was not solved. Perhaps she felt powerless. I know I did.

Time passed slowly. I wanted to move, to go for a drive, to consider the urge of putting an end to living. In the kitchen I found my parents sitting at the table, deep in conversation.

"Can I have the keys to the car? I need to go out and get something."

"Where are you going?" my father asked. It was the first time I saw his face since he had come home. I looked at him without really seeing him. I didn't want to see the worry in the lines across his forehead. I didn't want to make eye contact.

"Just to the drugstore."

My parents looked at each other, silently considering my request. I could see the wheels turning in their minds. Would it be better to hide the keys or to give me their trust?

At the drugstore, not far from my house, I perused the aisle that contained the sleeping pills. I picked up one bottle and then another. Frozen, I stared at them.

No, I heard a soft voice in my head. *No. Walk away.*

I moved away and found myself in the school supplies aisle. I picked out a new notebook and a pen. I paid for them at the cashier, left the drugstore and drove home.

Those may have been the most important thirty minutes of my life. Facing turmoil I could not even find the words to describe, I decided to stay. What was the gentle, invisible hand that guided me that night? Was it grace? Had it been nurtured and coaxed forward by Mrs. M.'s steadfast listening ear, by my parents' guarded trust? We never know how we save a life.

When I got home, I found my parents in exactly the same spot at the kitchen table. They watched me hang up the car keys on the hook by the back door. They pretended to be talking about other things, while holding vigil for a revelation that would not come that night.

We never spoke of this day again.

PILGRIM

It's October 1997, and the long Indian summer of Iberia has cast its last shadow. Hot days walking across the Pyrenees and the dusty plains of Northern Spain give way to days of rain.

After six hundred miles of walking, I am leaving Burgos on a cold morning. It is rush hour in the city. Cars and trucks fill the streets with a cacophony of sounds. Pedestrians walk briskly on their way to modern office buildings. Elegant Spanish women, about my age, pass me, leaving behind a mist of fresh, spicy perfume. I take in the scents. I miss smelling pretty.

I cross the street at the traffic light, my walking stick at my side, and stop in front of a shop window. I focus on my reflection. I am wearing a bright windbreaker, a hand-me-down from the Seattle to Portland bike race. It is a canvas of vibrant splotches: bright orange, yellow, red, green. The backpack straps permanently dent the jacket, now torn and repaired with orange duct tape. The darker roots of my hair push the dyed blond straight up and out of a bright pink fleece headband. Green long underwear leggings are bracketed by a pair of faded blue shorts and a pair of well-worn hiking boots. I hold the walking stick in front of me and lean on it with my gloved hands, in a now familiar rest pose.

A smile spreads across my lips. I barely recognize this clownish patchwork of colors. My eyes glow like stained glass windows kissed by a ray of sun. A gleeful laugh bursts out of me.

I do not have a photograph of this moment. There is no selfie to memorialize this encounter. "Remember this," I whisper to myself. "Remember this pure joy of meeting, as if for the first time, the one who has loved you since the beginning of time."

DISCOVERY

Before our first kiss, we held each other for hours, standing in the little kitchen of your apartment in Rabat. The muffled roar of mopeds and cars behind the windowpanes announced a new day in the capital city of Morocco. After cleaning up the breakfast dishes, we stood facing one another. Our bodies joined like magnets pressing against each other. Clothed, chest against chest, arms gently wrapped around each other's back, intertwined. I hadn't felt that before—my body fitting to another's easily, that sense of completeness, of finding home with another person.

We had words for what was blossoming. We didn't dare say them out loud. Is this what it meant to be gay, to be a lesbian, to be in love with a woman? If I said the words out loud, if I gave it a name, would it break the spell? Would it shatter like a pane of glass?

I didn't want to give it a name. I only wanted to be here with you, my body against your body, my hand holding your hand. Time had stopped. Except it hadn't. You were late for work. What would you say if they asked? We held back thoughts and words, kept them at bay behind the front door. There would be time enough for those later.

BLASPHEMY

I am eleven. I mark up the prayer books in the pew with the short pencils provided to write donation amounts on the envelopes for the collection basket. I circle words and underline phrases that I find problematic. I do this discreetly, with barely noticeable strokes of the pencil in my hand.

. . .

I squint while I watch the priest talk at the lectern. This magnifies my vision of the aura around his body—dancing shadows of light and darkness.

. . .

As an adult I seek a place and community of belonging. Where is the place where I can bring my whole self and experience the unconditional love of the divine?

. . .

Incense is intoxicating. I love "Feast Days," like Easter or Christmas when the priest comes up the aisle swinging the ornate metal ball of smoke. This musky, pungent smell adds intrigue to the mysteries.

In Medieval Europe the incense dispensers are enormous fumigators used to camouflage the odor of the multitude of unwashed bodies crammed into pews.

. . .

Shaman blow smoke to reveal truth.

. . .

The cathedral doors are always open, even when it's not time for mass. That is when I like to visit: in the liminal hours. I kneel at an interior chapel dedicated to Mary. Rows of candles separate me from her statue. "*Blessed art thou among women.*" I have lit many candles for loved ones, for myself, for the planet. Is that faith? The coins make a clinking sound when they drop into the metal box to pay for the candles. I leave a little light in cathedrals in France and Spain along the route to Compostela.

. . .

"Maman, I lit a candle for you at the Cathedral of Notre Dame," I tell my mother on the phone, after a trip to France.

"Merci," she says quietly, a note of reverence sounds in her voice.

. . .

My mother goes to a church near her house in a parish outside of Washington, DC. It sits in a cul-de-sac of conservatism in an otherwise progressive part of Maryland. The folding table of "Right to Life" pamphlets in the foyer irritate her. Maman describes to me over the phone her encounter with a lady from behind the table who reaches out to offer her a pamphlet. My mother shows her the flat palm of her hand as she waves the pamphlet away with a crisp, "No, thank you."

One year the ladies in the foyer have a petition for parishioners to sign in support of a law that would deny gay people the right to marry. The ladies hold out the petition as people come into church. My mother describes to me how she tries to avoid them. She walks briskly past them.

"Last Sunday a lady followed me all the way to the pew where I was going to sit." Maman is shocked at the audacity of the church lady's persistence. "She said, 'Don't you want to sign this?' And thrust the petition towards me."

I imagine the piercing look she gives the woman in the pause before she responds.

"What would you do if your daughter was gay?" she asks the woman.

I am dumbfounded at my mother's bold retort. And in church! "What did she say?" I ask.

"Nothing. She looked down and walked back to the table in the foyer."

"Why do you keep going to *that* church," I ask my mother, worried that she is in enemy territory. "There are other churches you could go to nearby."

"I go to be alone with my thoughts and with God," she says. After a pause, she chuckles, "And, they have good parking."

A LESBIAN WAS HERE

1.

When we worked for the government in Washington, DC, and acquaintances asked us what we had done over the weekend, we carefully avoided saying each other's names or using "she" and "her." Casual revelations seemed dangerous.

2.

For several years, I was "the woman you owned a car with."

3.

I remember the sheet of stickers I bought at the feminist bookstore in Amherst, Massachusetts, where we lived after we left Washington, DC. The stickers were purple dots an inch in diameter. The words, *A Lesbian Was Here,* were printed on each one. I imagined how I would gleefully stick them in random places at rest stops on our drive across the country.

4.

We only used one sticker. It was at Wall Drug, in South Dakota. After eating an ice cream cone and perusing the tacky tourist shops, I went to the restroom before we got back on the road. I managed to stick *A Lesbian Was Here* on the inside of the restroom stall. Heart pounding, hands shaking, I ran back to the car where you waited, engine running, like the desperados' getaway car. I don't think I washed my hands.

5.

The woman at the front desk at the motel in Billings, Montana, asked us, "Y'all twins?"

You made a joke, "No. But we've been traveling for so long that we might start to look like each other, just like people start to look like their pets." She chuckled and handed us the plastic diamond key, with the room number stamped on it. Your humor saved us more than once.

6.

The next morning, we had breakfast in a diner. We noticed we were the only two women in the place who had short hair. Every other woman had long hair, blow dried, curled up, sprayed into place. I remember how people stared at us.

7.

At your aunt and uncle's house in Bountiful, Utah, we stayed in a room with two small twin beds. The walls were adorned with crucifixes. There were statues of the Virgin Mary. We had gone for a hike with your retired uncle and aunt. They had talked about how hard it had been to be Catholic in Mormon-dominated Salt Lake City. Your cousins came over for a barbecue. The next morning, we were repacking our Subaru hatchback in the driveway. Your aunt paused, as if she had forgotten something, and asked, "Whose car is this?" I guess she wanted to know if it was yours or mine. "It's our car," you said. "Oh," she said.

8.

I remember how it felt to hold your hand as we walked down Broadway in Capitol Hill in Seattle, the "gay" part of town. It felt like the first time, allowing our fingers to interlace for blocks at a time without the constant reflex to let go in case someone was watching. The vigilance never quite wore off.

9.

We listened to NPR on the radio as we drove. Sometimes it would fade out in a snowstorm of static. We turned the radio off and held our breath. Contact with friendly voices was lost. Then when the radio did get a signal, it brought us parts of speeches from the Republican National Convention. It was 1992. "*Family values, blah, blah, blah. Homosexuals, blah, blah, blah.*" We turned the radio off again. Watching the monotonous flat land on either side of the highway was preferable to listening to politicians proselytizing hate.

10.

I remember how we stayed on women-owned land in Montana. The woman who greeted us told us, "Pull your rig on up." We looked back at our two-door hatchback and wondered if she was talking to us. There was nobody else around, so it was us. I thought rigs needed to be at least the size of a truck. For years we continued to call our little Subaru our "rig," and giggled each time.

11.

We were so excited to stay in a real teepee on this land. We had not planned for the rain. I found myself standing buck naked outside the teepee in the middle of the night, reaching high to close its top flap to stop the rain from pouring onto our sleeping bags. I remember thinking, *I may not be cut out for this kind of travel.*

12.

The catalytic converter gave up the ghost as we roared into Indianapolis. Luckily, we had planned to stay with our friend Claire. Her dad helped us get the car into a shop. It was the first time I had even heard about this car part; it was not in our budget. Claire's floor was hard but cozy. The price was right. And her dad was delighted to help the two women with their car.

806 MILES
(AFTER CHEN CHEN)

With a twenty-two-pound backpack. Without knowing if I'd packed too much or too little. With knowing the beginning, Le Puy-en-Velay, in France, and the end point, Santiago de Compostela, in Spain. Without knowing what would happen in between on the 806-mile walking journey. With tearing out the pages of the guidebook we no longer needed because each extra ounce carried matters. Without a smart phone in 1997. With blisters on my feet and cramps in my legs. Without knowing where we would lay our heads to sleep each night. Without clean sheets and a good mattress. With being the stranger, *estrangera*. Without a title or job. With *Pelegrina*, "Pilgrim," a new greeting on the journey. Without selfies. With a camera to photograph villages, prairies, cows, sheep, dusty plains, the tops of mountains, and faces, so many faces. Without notifications or texts. With hospitality and welcome and rediscovered love of humanity. With understanding that the outer journey is manifestation of inner transformation. With arriving.

Compostela pilgrimage, 1997

PIERCED STONE

The veil is thin here. If there are passageways between the dimensions, surely they are in these stones, perched atop a cliff in the Pyrenees. I scratch the dirt with my fingernails and taste it on my tongue. Was this the soil that nourished my ancestors? Was this the once-soaked mud and ash that delivered them home?

I am at Peyrepertuse, the remains of a thirteenth-century fortress that served to protect a band of Cathars. They were the devotees, prefects, men and women, leaders of the ancient religion. They were herdsmen and farmers, seamstresses, potters. They were villagers and craftspeople supported by local noblemen who protected them for as long they could from the bloodthirsty army of the Pope. It was the Inquisition. The Cathars were hunted "heretics."

When I first learned about the Cathars, in my thirties, I wondered if there was a connection between my mother's ancestry and this early religious sect that thrived in south-central France and northern Spain. I studied and read all I could about this lost band of believers. I never asked my family for fear that I might be ridiculed as a "new age" seeker in search of a holy grail. Genocide shatters and distorts the memory stored in our DNA. How many generations does it take to be rid of the silence and twisted shame? The more I learned and traveled to the region and the sites where the Cathars were besieged by the Pope's army, the more I experienced the resonance in my bones.

In 2016, while visiting family in France, a cousin and I met for ice cream. We were waiting for her bus to take her back to her apartment. Out of the blue, she turned to me and said, "Papé was Cathar."

"What?" I asked, unsure if I had heard her correctly.

"Our grandfather was Cathar," she repeated. I held her gaze, searching her eyes for clues. Was she kidding? In the forty-plus years we had known each other, we had never talked about this.

Her words clicked into place like the missing piece of a puzzle.

What did it mean for a man to be Cathar in the twentieth century? The beliefs and practices were long expunged in the thirteenth century pyres of burned humans. What difference had this made to our grandfather? Did he inherit an unspoken trauma? Could this help explain his infamous angry temper, his tyranny over his children? That day was the first time I had ever heard the word, Cathar, spoken by a family member.

History is written by the victors. Accounts from the point of view of the Cathars are hard to find. Only the leaders of the sect, male and female, were literate.

I rely on the stirring of my blood essence and the resonance in my bones to know the truth of my ancestors.

On the top of Peyrepertuse, the ruined Cathar castle in France, I hear the footsteps beyond the veil. I hear the distant clanging of livestock grazing in the hills, the calls of the shepherdess guiding her flock. I hear the cries of my ancestors to live as they had lived for hundreds of years and to believe the pure story of their place in humanity.

IV.

FULL MOON

During a penumbral eclipse a portion of the moon's surface is obscured by the Earth's shadow. We know it's there, yet in that moment, we can't see it. There was a penumbral eclipse on the day I was born.

. . .

When I turned forty, my mother told me I had been born on the "Whites Only" floor of the Columbia Hospital for Women in Washington, DC. We were spending time together that summer. She dropped that fact out of the blue at dinner one day. We were eating soup. When she said those words, my spoon fell out of my hands, splattering broth on my glasses and on the tablecloth around my bowl.

I looked at her, unable to speak.

"We didn't have a choice," she said. "They just sent us to that part of the hospital. It's just the way it was."

In that moment, the idea I had of myself and my family not participating in the racism all around us, collapsed like a house of cards. Even in the very act of my being born I could not escape the ideology of white supremacy that underpins the society into which I arrived. I felt a mix of betrayal and culpability. Betrayal because I had not asked to be separated from the Black and brown babies in the hospital that day. Culpability because I benefited from privileges simply because I was a white baby coming into the world.

July 1962. John Fitzgerald Kennedy was president of the United States. The basements of Washington's public schools were quietly being outfitted into bomb shelters. The Cuban Missile crisis was only a few months away. These facts I later learned in school. What was not part of the curriculum, was the fact that in that year, white and Black babies were still separated at birth.

As a child I was naturally curious about my birth. Over the years my mother shared that story through her occasional musings. She shared disconnected anecdotes that shaped my sense of the moment. Like the one about her doctor, Dr. Kuhn, whom she may have visited twice during her surprise pregnancy. He had guessed that her baby would be born on Bastille Day, July 14.

"That would be perfect for a French girl like you," he said, cigarette dangling from his lips.

"His ashtray was full of cigarette butts," my mother told me once. That was not uncommon in those days.

As it turns out, I was born a few days after Bastille Day. I pieced together that this was probably better for my father's schedule. Bastille Day had landed on a Saturday, and he would have been working late serving customers at the French restaurant where he worked.

In 1962, French cuisine was all the rage in Washington, thanks to Julia Child's famous cookbook. French restaurants were popping up all over town and there was a high demand for young, handsome men with charming Gallic accents. "So authentic!" Perhaps the tips were more generous.

My mother had to quit her waitressing job a few months before I was born. Le Père François, which is what the staff called the proprietor of the French restaurant where she worked, did not want his "girls" to appear pregnant to the diners.

These were the snippets of stories that I had gathered over the years about my birth. The one additional puzzle piece of information that my mother added on my fortieth birthday revealed a complexity I had not yet perceived. Like the phases of the penumbral eclipse that day in 1962, something that was in the shadows, and paradoxically very present the whole time, was revealed.

HAIR

When our biracial daughter was a toddler, and her full head of hair had come in, older white ladies would stop us in parking garages as I pushed her in her stroller to the car. They would look at her light brown, olive-tinted skin; her head of dark curls; her bright, coal black eyes and then look at me and fixate on my mane of long blond curls. They'd comment, in a lilting, sing song voice, "We know where she got her hair."

If I had been a cartoon character, the thought bubble over my head would read, "We actually have no idea where she got her hair!" My partner and I did not know the dark, curly hair side of our daughter's Black heritage. The conversation about her birth story was not one I wanted to have with the much too friendly stranger in the parking garage as I fastened this bubbly toddler into her car seat.

"Isn't that interesting?" I'd say, through my forced smile. "Yup, we both have curly hair."

Most of the time I sensed that they meant well. Here we were, mother and daughter, my golden pink Caucasian skin to her *café au lait* biracial tones; her coal dark eyes to my hazel eyes; her soft black locks around her face and my full mane of curly blond curls. People seemed to want so much to see our similarities, to detect where our gene pools aligned. So they focused on the hair, and exclaimed, as if reassured to have found the solution to the puzzle, the one thing that was like the other, appeasing their concern. Indeed, we did belong together.

At sixteen, my daughter now towers over me. She still has her dark brown curls. My hair is whiter and still curly. That much has not changed. The cuteness of the mom pushing the stroller of a chirping toddler is no longer there. I wonder what people see when they notice us at the bus stop in the morning waiting for our respective buses. At first glance, do people see two strangers—one mixed-race teenage girl, one middle-aged white woman? We are incognito. Our connection need not be revealed. Our love is weathered like the soft leather of a favorite bag—familiar, flexible, worn in spots, and enduring.

GUARDIANS

There is a framed photograph in our dining room taken by an AP photographer at a press conference in Olympia, the Washington state capital. I have it memorized. I am wearing a black blazer with white stitching and black pants. Peg, my partner, is wearing a similar "business casual" outfit. Our daughter stands between us in her favorite velvety red dress with sparkles. She is holding her stuffed puppy in one hand and holding Peg's wrist in the other. She leans back and looks up at Peg, whose arm is around her small torso. She is gazing into Peg's eyes. Maybe she has asked Peg a question. Peg is holding her gaze, steadying her in this intimate moment under the flash of cameras and extended microphones outside of the picture. Our daughter is seven years old. It is January 23, 2012, a crisp, cloudless day.

On that day, we are up before dawn. Our friend Mike drives us to Olympia, ninety minutes away. He, too, is prepared to speak to our legislators about what marriage equality means to him. We are nervous about arriving at the state capitol alone, and feel more secure accompanied by this tall, elegant man, former military. We had been warned that we would be outnumbered by the people on the other side of the issue—those who would testify passionately against marriage equality. We don't want our daughter to be harassed or taunted by people who don't respect us.

We pass through the quiet, cold steps of the majestic capitol building into the din of the entry hall. It is crowded with people, most of whom have arrived in buses provided by their churches, to lobby representatives and testify against gay marriage.

Our small group, those of us who are here to testify for gay marriage, are checked in quickly and escorted to a conference room. There is a table with orange juice and donuts, crayons, and sheets of coloring pages. Legislative aides explain how the day will go. We would probably be called up to speak but nothing is certain. "You can't predict how these things go," they alert us. Prepared to pass the time, we have packed our daughter's favorite books, her DVD player and headphones, and snacks in a grocery bag. Democracy involves a lot of waiting.

"Please let us know if you need anything," the press manager says, smiling and looking each of us in the eyes. We nod in thanks and smile.

The legislative chamber is at capacity, so we spend the morning watching testimonies on television screens in a large overflow room. At one point, as the room fills with people prepared to testify on both sides of the issue, a capitol security officer asks for our attention and explains in a stern voice how we are to behave. No shouting at others in the room or at the television screens. Keep our voices low and be respectful. He lets us know that anyone behaving in a harassing or disrespectful manner will be asked to leave. Finally, he points out where the bathrooms are. I am grateful that this official has provided guidelines because I feel exposed in close quarters with people who use hateful words about families like mine. We shuttle our bag of games, juice boxes, and sandwiches to three seats together near the front. We try to sit where we recognize people friendly to our cause: young gay men in suits, a woman pastor I recognize from a church I had gone to a couple of times. I want to create a moat of protection around us on the folding chairs.

More of the people from the buses are checked in and arrive to look for seats in the room with us. Some wear black buttons with white symbols for marriage between one man and one woman that look like the symbols indicating gendered restrooms. Our daughter notices this and asks us why people are wearing "bathroom buttons." We smile quietly.

We wait for hours, holding our breath each time a testimony against gay marriage is made on the television screen. We are glad that our daughter has her headset on to watch movies. I am on guard for any unkind words or arguments in our vicinity. I turn around once to ask someone to be quiet as he practices reading from his note card, his argument against marriage equality rolling out at high volume.

His voice quiets. We offer snacks to anyone around us, especially the children.

The minister from the Unitarian Universalist Church, who I recognize, is passing out buttons and stickers that say, "Standing on the Side of Love." They are symbols of support. She gives me a handful and I pass them around. I put one or two on my jacket. Our daughter puts one on her dress. I find comfort in this bright button. It represents an antidote to the animosity I feel in the room. Two little girls, close to our daughter's age, are sitting in front of us and turn to watch our excitement about the buttons. They reach their hands out asking if they can have one. I see that they are with their mom, who is not here to support marriage equality.

"You have to ask your mom first," I whisper.

They look at their mother, who keeps her back to us. She turns toward the little girls and shakes her head to indicate, "No." The children glance back at me. I shrug my shoulders and make an expression of regret on my face. They lower their eyes and turn around to face the front of the room as their mother has asked.

In the afternoon, we are invited to come into the legislative chamber to give our testimony. We wait our turn behind a mix of people who have come to give their opinions about gay marriage. I feel my blood boil and notice the shake that overcomes my body as I listen to people opine to our elected representatives that gay marriage, and therefore my relationship and my family, are wrong. In those moments I hold my daughter close to me and squeeze her hand. We had told her that there may be a moment when she would be asked to speak. Sitting on the living room couch the evening before she had shared a version of what she might say on the legislative floor.

I gaze outside the window at the clear blue sky and the rolling green hills of the capitol grounds. I breathe. I steady myself. The group of three people who speak just before us are white men: a rabbi and two pastors. In contrast to the Catholic archbishop I heard speak earlier in the day, these men speak in support of marriage equality—affirming the love and dignity of all people. I am grateful for their loving words spoken from the authority their positions grant them.

We take our seats. I glance up at the panel of lawmakers in front of us. They are seated behind desks on a tiered riser. Their faces are inscrutable and from that height they look like a wall of inquisitors. I shake that image away and focus on the legislator who I know is a gay dad. I decide that when my turn comes, I will speak directly to him. The green light blinks to signal that our allotted time has begun. Peg speaks first and I continue, offering a two-and-a-half-minute summary of the last twenty-six years of our lives together. Meeting as Peace Corps volunteers, getting married in Portland and having our marriage later voided, while at the same time becoming parents, our love for our child, our worry about the lack of practical protections that marriage offers families and children. It was a lot to pack in. Thirty seconds remain and we turn to our daughter and ask if there is anything she wants to share.

She stretches her arm out slowly to reach for the microphone. She speaks from her heart, no notecards needed. "It makes me feel sad," she begins. "It makes me feel like there is a crater in my heart." Peg gently puts her hand over hers as she continues to hold the microphone. "I know my moms love each other," she continues, "so they should be able to get married. It's not fair."

The light turns red. Our time is up. We gather ourselves, offer smiles of thanks to the representatives, and exit as the next speakers step up.

We return to the din of the crowded hall outside the chamber. My daughter is thirsty and asks for a drink of water. As I escort her to the water fountain, we pass three young white girls playing on and around a railing. They stop to whisper and point at us. I stand between these girls and my Black daughter as she leans over the stream of water to drink. She looks so fragile and innocent, like a bird quenching her thirst. I feel a surge of protection for her, guardianship in its purest sense. I have the sensation of invisible wings on my back unfurling to their widest wingspan. Love, like water, is our birthright.

The sun begins to descend on the horizon of this long day. The room where we had waited shows the signs of nervous people and bored children: empty juice boxes and blunt crayons are scattered on the carpet. The trashcan overflows with the remains of box lunches. We pack up our grocery bag, gather our coats, and walk across the vast hall we had entered that morning. This time it is emptying out as people head to their waiting cars and buses.

As we reach the front doors, a woman stops us. I recognize her as one of the organizers from the opposing side.

"You are such a beautiful family, I just want to say," she says, with a tentative smile.

In the one-second pause before responding, I wonder: *Was this an apology? Was it a "hate the sin; love the sinner" moment? Was she looking for my blessing? My forgiveness?*

I manage a nod of acknowledgment. It is time for our sweet, brave family to find our friend Mike and go home.

WHITE MOMMAS (2014)

1.

Black and brown faces turn towards us. Our daughter finds a desk and disappears into the classroom of children that look like her.

2.

Black children, brown children, excluded from the class field trip. Is it just a coincidence?

3.

"Too unpredictable," said the teacher.

"Like a circle that doesn't fit in a square," said the principal. "We're sorry, she must stay behind with the other children who cannot go."

"It'll be okay," said the vice principal, an officious attempt at comfort, while our eyes welled up with tears.

4.

How did we allow this to happen? Why did we not protest even more? Why did we not scream?

5.

The situation called for yelling. The situation called for rage.

Expressed.

Unbridled.

To strip the blinders off.

6.

"We'll call a lawyer," we said the following year, at the first hint of exclusion.

7.

They did not call our bluff. Our brown daughter went on the field trip.

8.

"She is a natural leader," they said, surprised at how talented the circle was in a crowd of squares.

"We know," we said, "She thrives in outdoor settings like the one she was denied last year."

9.

At the end of the field trip the math wiz, a boy, punched another boy in the nose.

"So out of character," they said.

10.

No one saw *that* coming.

PRAYERS

After my father died, I started to memorize poems and recite them on long walks by the lake near where I live.

I don't remember how it started exactly. The stringing together of images, sounds, and syllables recited out loud filled the ache left by loss. I would copy out a poem on a piece of paper, fold it, and put it in my pocket for my walk. I took the paper out, read a line, and repeated it over and over. I learned the poems, sound by sound, word by word, line by line. I memorized the images and words to the cadence of my steps along the footpath. These poems are like gemstones. They hold vibrations of healing, of love, of forgiveness. They are like the talismans of old to guide me as the mysteries of life unfold. For a few years I recited poems at gatherings, for birthdays mostly—sending little gifts of words and vibration into the world.

These gemstones live in my mind now. This morning, I was awakened in the early hours by worry about my teenage daughter, who is officially almost an adult. That's terrifying. I brought myself to the couch with my cup of tea and sat down in the quiet hours of the early morning when the blanket of night still covers the city. I wished that my father were alive so that I could ask for his advice. And a gemstone appeared in my mind, the first few words of a poem. I see myself walking on the footpath to the lake, reciting those words to the rhythm of my steps.

I will not solve the problems of the world this morning. I will not find the one solution that will quell my daughter's suffering. These poems that dwell in my mind are my prayers: hope, acceptance, healing, and love. Maybe my father planted them there when he left and now, they have grown into trees.

ONE PART SUGAR, FOUR PARTS WATER

I have become a bird lady. It started a few years ago when I hung a bird feeder in the cherry tree outside the window over the kitchen sink. Then I added a suet cake. The point of no return was when the hummingbird feeder appeared. It hangs right outside the other kitchen window on a plant hook. I can open the widow to reach it and easily bring it inside to refill. I make the solution in batches, diluting the sugar in water in a pan over low heat on the stove. I store the unused portion in a glass jar in the fridge.

This week it's arctic cold in Seattle. It's another 2021 record-setting weather event, and the hummingbird food is frozen outside my window. At first light, I bring it inside and defrost it by holding the feeder in my hands. The slushy sugary stuff slowly turns to liquid again and I rehang the feeder on the hook. I do this throughout the day, defrosting and rehanging.

I've named the hummingbird, or hummingbirds, Kiki. I have seen two of them vehemently guard this feeder. I can't tell them apart. They dive bomb each other when one is feeding and only rarely sip at the same time. Kiki flutters outside my window, their wings a blur over the feeder as I reattach it to the hook. They alight for a moment and push their long beak into a small hole on the feeder. Their long tongue, like a thread, laps up the ice-cold liquid.

"We've disrupted their eco-system," I tell Peg. I suspect I've repeated this several times, but she is kind and just nods.

"We have to keep feeding them, especially in the winter when food sources are scarce, or they'll die," I say.

One part sugar, four parts water. I can't bear the thought of a still hummingbird body on the frozen ground. If only saving the planet were this simple.

PLANTING INSTRUCTIONS

The canna plants in my backyard are from my mother who lives in Maryland more than three thousand miles away. She pulled three new shoots from the thick patch in her front bed and put them, roots first, in a plastic bag.

"Take these back with you. Plant them in your yard. They make nice red flowers. *Tu verras*, you'll see, and by next year they will spread. I have lots." She waves towards the high stems outside her front door.

I pick up the plastic drugstore bag and consider how I will stuff these tender shoots into my carry-on for the cross-country flight back to Seattle.

"Do you think, they'll make it?" I ask doubtfully, looking from the bag to my mother.

"Of course; they're hardy," she shrugs. "*Tu verras*," she says, her hands in motion. "And if one doesn't make it, there are two others."

She makes it sound so easy. But I know better. Plants die in my yard all the time.

My mother is a confident gardener. Passersby slow down and admire her bountiful perennial beds.

If she happens to be outside, puttering and weeding, people exclaim, "Your yard is so beautiful."

"Tank you, iz noting, you know," she shrugs her shoulders and smiles. After more than sixty years of speaking English, the "h" is still silent, like in French.

We have video chats every couple of weeks. She is obsessed with talking about politics and gives me a run down on all the news she listens to as if I had not already heard it. Even though we agree on most issues, I look for ways to change the topic.

"The canna has flowered," I announce, thrilled to report a garden victory. "Now what should I do in the fall?"

"Just cut the stems way back and protect them. They'll come back in the spring. You'll see, you'll have even more."

After I first came out as a gay, my mother didn't want to talk about that part of my life. She didn't want to talk about or see "that woman," ever again. Our relationship was strained, almost to the breaking point.

It seems like a whole chapter went missing. It was the chapter where I imagine mothers show their daughters how to establish a household, how to nurture a marriage. That part, even if it's fairy tale, that part never happened.

My mother knows about transplanting. She planted herself thousands of miles away from the warm Mediterranean soil that nurtured her, far away from her mother's attention. I also have, like these canna shoots, re-rooted myself and thrived.

"Make sure you water them every day until they take root. They like plenty of sun," she repeats to me as I wait for the Uber to take me to the airport.

My mother speaks her care through the tender canna shoots. She was right—they are about to bloom again. I tend to them carefully, as they take root in a soil so foreign to the one they have thrived in.

HOW TO WATCH TIKTOK VIDEOS WITH YOUR DAUGHTER

1. As soon as you hear, "Mom, I have some videos for you to watch," take a deep breath.

2. Press the pause button on your internal dialogue, *These videos are inane! What's happening to this generation?*

3. Remember this is "connection." She is seventeen years old and still wants to spend time with you. She wants to share what matters to her in this moment.

4. Squint, if you must, to ease the suffering. Especially when the sound is on and the rapid stream of exaggerated accents and strange voices accompany the fast flickering of dogs or people doing weird, and often vulgar, things.

5. Don't ask questions. It'll be over fast.

6. Find one thing to appreciate and comment on: how the dog does remind you of your dog, for example. Don't pretend. She can tell.

7. Let her know when you are reaching your capacity. Say something like, "Okay, I only have energy for one more."

8. Don't bolt. Instead, when the viewing session is over, slowly unfold from the shoulder-to-shoulder huddle over the phone she is holding. Take a moment to take her in from head to toe. Appreciate her quietly. Smile on the inside. But don't make it weird.

9. When she refers to the TikTok universe, as "we," hide your internal cringe. Wonder how this new cohort of humans makes sense of this world.

10. Don't judge. Remember: they bear the burden of a planet on fire.

DAILY BREAD

"*Allahu Akbar, Allahu Akbar,*" the voice calls over the scratchy loudspeaker: a long line of pleading notes rise and fall, proclaiming, "God is Greatest, God is Greatest."

It always begins this way, the first words from a Koranic verse. Five times each day the muezzin chants from the mosque up the street from my house in the Moroccan town. His voice resonates with the calls from other mosques inside the walled city, creating a synchronized network of voices.

People stop what they are doing. The world slows down for a moment.

Some nights the call gently stirs me awake. Melodic verses rise and wash over the desert town under the carpet of stars in the night sky. It is a comforting sound in the deep, dark night, a reminder that someone keeps watch, assuring me again that we are part of a vast mystery.

. . .

Donnez-nous aujourd'hui notre pain de ce jour. "Give us this day our daily bread."

Each day, on the walking pilgrimage to Santiago de Compostela, I buy a baguette at the beginning of the day and strap it to my backpack. The daily bread, a promise and gift of sustenance when I need it: a snack with a square of chocolate, for lunch with fresh tomatoes, or by itself to nibble on while walking until we arrive at the next town.

. . .

What sustains twenty-first century humans? What is our pure source of nourishment as we plant the seeds for the recreation of the earth, our home?

ARRIVING

The country road gives way to urban sprawl as we approach Santiago de Compostela. Cars and trucks whiz by at speeds that are disorienting after walking the *Camino* for eleven weeks. The rush of pedestrians and vehicles causes us to unconsciously quicken our strides on the sidewalk along the busy city streets.

First stop: the cathedral to see the statue of Saint James, for whom this pilgrimage is named. Then to the archbishop's office to receive our certificates. We join the multitudes who have passed through these doors over the last thousand years. We are part of the collective of seekers motivated by reasons as diverse as the languages we speak and the lands from which we come.

At the archbishop's office we recognize two Flemish men we had met at one of the pilgrims' hostels. We had shared a simple meal while our socks dried in front of the fireplace. Now they are also collecting their certificates. The young woman behind the counter carefully and unceremoniously fills out a certificate for each of us in Latin. We admire them and take pictures of each other holding our certificates. Then it's time to say farewell.

"Have a good life," Hans says.

"See you in heaven," Lucas adds, "And if you get there and you don't see us there, know that we are still on the road."

"*Buen Camino*," I reply, in the now familiar pilgrims' greeting.

That was twenty-five years ago. I am still on the road.

Heaven *can* exist on earth.

Each day is another chance.

We can't wait.

Heaven is up to us.

Here.

Now.

ACKNOWLEDGMENTS

I n gratitude to so many, in no particular order:

To Darien Hsu Gee, editor of the Hali'a Aloha Series, and to the editorial team at Legacy Isle Publishing. Your compassionate, clear-eyed reading and generous feedback along the way helps turn dreams of publishing into reality. Thank you for believing.

To Peg, for a shared life of beauty and profound love. I wouldn't change a thing. Thanks for your patience and grace during this solo inner journey of a writer's process and for helping me get this project over the finish line.

To Ariana, holy one, most precious gift. Your courage and perseverance leave me in awe. Thanks for being one of my greatest teachers.

To the village of aunties, friends, neighbors, godparents who offer love, support, casseroles, laughter, kind and reassuring words on the adventure of parenting.

To author friends: Julie Dargis, Kristin Marra, Susan Forest, Lisa Voisin, Susan Hyatt, Posy Gering,

Kip Robinson Greenthal, Wendy Palmer, who modeled devotion to book projects from beginning to end. Thank you for inspiration from inception to manifestation.

To my freshmen students in the Writing Program at University of Massachusetts, you have no idea how your bold, raw stories offered tentatively on the page, coaxed me to unlock my own.

To the women of my generation and the generation before me who, while not always welcome, busted down the doors of the "canon" to add their experience and voices to academic education.

To my colleagues in my spiritual community, Training in Power Academy. Thank you for your abiding companionship in the creation and manifestation of heaven on earth.

To my family in the US and in France, thank you for shaping me and nurturing me. Your stories live in my bones.

ALEX GARLAND

Catherine has been traversing cultures all her life. Born in Washington, DC, to French parents, she learned English on the kindergarten playground. Bicultural and bilingual from birth, she often finds herself in between worlds. Growing up, she journeyed between France and the US, graduating from Georgetown University with a degree in French. She taught English in Morocco as a Peace Corps volunteer, and taught writing at the University of Massachusetts. Catherine holds a MEd in International Education from the University of Massachusetts, an MA in Organizational Leadership from Seattle University, and certification as a Leadership Embodiment coach. Catherine is an executive coach at the University of Washington and teaches meditation through Training in Power Academy. Catherine celebrates her deep love of France by flipping crêpes every year on Chandeleur with her family and friends. She shares her life with her wife and daughter and their two chihuahuas in Seattle, Washington.

CPSIA information can be obtained
at www.ICGtesting.com
Printed in the USA
BVHW091512200922
647490BV00013B/1072